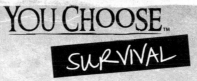

YOU CHOOSE™

SURVIVAL

Can You Survive

AN EARTHQUAKE?

An Interactive Survival Adventure

Rachael Hanel

Raintree is an imprint of Capstone Global Library Limited, a company incorporated in England and Wales having its registered office at 7 Pilgrim Street, London, EC4V 6LB – Registered company number: 6695582

www.raintreepublishers.co.uk
myorders@raintreepublishers.co.uk

Text © Capstone Global Library Limited 2012
This edition published in 2015
The moral rights of the proprietor have been asserted.

Edited by Angie Kaelberer
Designed by Gene Bentdahl
Picture research by Wanda Winch
Production by Helen McCreath
Printed and bound in China

ISBN 978 1 406 27994 8
18 17 16 15 14
10 9 8 7 6 5 4 3 2 1

British Library Cataloguing in Publication Data
A full catalogue record for this book is available from the British Library.

Acknowledgements
We would like to thank the following for permission to reproduce photographs:
Alamy: Aflo Foto Agency, 89, Damon Coulter, 78; AP Images: Damian Dovarganes, 11; Corbis: AP/ Shuji Kajiyama, 90, Bettmann, 33, 53, Jim Sugar, 48, Nippon News/AFLO/Mainichi Newspaper, 83, Nippon News/AFLO/Tetsurou Chiharada, 26; Dreamstime: Walter Graneri, cover; iStockphoto Inc: Skip ODonnell, 103; Newscom: EFE/Leo La Valle, 100, Zuma Press, 65 Zuma Press/Les Stone, 57; Shutterstock: Darrenp, 6, FloridaStock, 14, kropic1, 44, MaxFX, 16, Radu Razvan, 74, Spirit of America, 35, 73, Tom Wang, 19; Wikipedia: David Eccles (gringer), 8

We would like to thank April Kelcy, Emergency Management Consultant in Earthquake Solutions, for her invaluable help in the preparation of this book.

Every effort has been made to contact copyright holders of material reproduced in this book. Any omissions will be rectified in subsequent printings if notice is given to the publisher.

All the Internet addresses (URLs) given in this book were valid at the time of going to press. However, due to the dynamic nature of the Internet, some addresses may have changed, or sites may have changed or ceased to exist since publication. While the author and publisher regret any inconvenience this may cause readers, no responsibility for any such changes can be accepted by either the author or the publisher.

CONTENTS

About your
ADVENTURE

YOU are about to experience one of the most unpredictable events in nature – an earthquake! You have no warning. How will you stay alive?

In this book you'll deal with extreme survival situations. You'll explore how the knowledge you have and the choices you make can mean the difference between life and death.

Chapter one sets the scene. Then you choose which path to read. Follow the directions at the bottom of each page. The choices you make will change your outcome. After you finish one path, go back and read the others for new perspectives and more adventures.

YOU CHOOSE the path
you take through your adventure.

Earthquakes strike without warning and can cause enormous damage.

An unpredictable moment

Imagine a bright, sunny day. People are outside walking, running or relaxing. Then without warning, the ground starts to shake. Trees topple and buildings crumble. People panic and scream. The shaking lasts only moments, but the entire landscape changes.

Earthquakes strike with little warning. Unlike other natural disasters such as hurricanes and tornadoes, there's nothing to see before they occur.

Earthquakes strike when tectonic plates below Earth's surface shift and move. Most earthquakes occur at fault lines – the places where the tectonic plates intersect.

Turn the page.

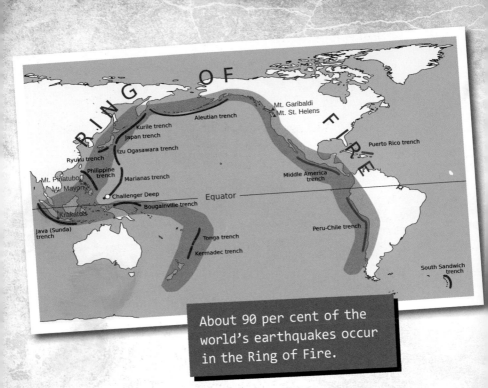

RING OF FIRE

Mt. Garibaldi
Mt. St. Helens

Aleutian trench

Kurile trench

Japan trench

Izu Ogasawara trench

Ryuku trench

Philippine trench

Mt. Pinatubo

Mt. Mayon

Marianas trench

Challenger Deep

Bougainville trench

Krakatoa

Java (Sunda) trench

Tonga trench

Kermadec trench

Middle America trench

Puerto Rico trench

Peru-Chile trench

South Sandwich trench

Equator

About 90 per cent of the world's earthquakes occur in the Ring of Fire.

Earthquakes are more likely to happen in the Ring of Fire. This area is around the edges of the Pacific Ocean. It includes Japan, Indonesia and the coasts of Alaska, Chile and the United States.

But even locations far away from the ocean can experience big earthquakes. The New Madrid fault system in the United States runs 150 miles from Illinois to Tennessee, also affecting parts of Indiana, Missouri, Arkansas, Kentucky and Mississippi. South Carolina also has a major fault line. Around the world, earthquakes strike along fault lines in the Arabian Peninsula, east Africa and the Mediterranean Sea.

Earthquakes are measured on the Richter scale. The strongest earthquakes have measured more than 9.0. These include measurements of 9.5 in Chile in 1960, 9.2 in Alaska, USA, in 1964 and 9.1 off the coast of Sumatra in 2004.

Because earthquakes can strike without warning, it is important to have a disaster plan in place. The British Geological Survey distributes information about what to do before, during and after an earthquake.

Turn the page.

If you live in an earthquake region, make sure your home is safe. Falling household objects often injure people. Make sure pictures and mirrors are securely fastened to walls. Secure top-heavy furniture to wall studs with the use of brackets. Tie down TVs and computer monitors with nylon straps or buckles that can be easily removed and relocated.

Create an emergency plan. Will you know where to reunite with family and friends in case you get separated? Keep a torch and shoes near your bed, in case an earthquake occurs during the night. You should make sure your torch is safe to use. Some torches have been tested in dangerous conditions and will not give off sparks that could trigger gas explosions. Families in earthquake areas should have disaster kits. These kits include medicine, bottled water, snacks, batteries, a battery-operated radio and heavy-duty plastic bags.

The USGS recommends the "drop, cover and hold on" action when an earthquake strikes.

The USGS also offers suggestions for how to protect yourself when an earthquake starts. If you are indoors, drop, cover and hold on. Get under a sturdy piece of furniture. If you can't do that, stay by an interior wall and protect your head and neck with your arms. Don't go outside until you are sure the earthquake is over.

Turn the page.

If you are caught outside, get to an open area. Avoid pavements or areas near tall buildings. If you are in a car, pull over to the side of the road as soon as possible and stay in the car. Avoid bridges and overpasses, because they might collapse. If you're near the sea, try to find higher ground after the initial shaking stops. Earthquakes can trigger huge waves called tsunamis.

Once it is safe to get up, move carefully so that you don't trip over fallen objects or run into debris hanging from the ceiling. It's usually best to leave the building and go and find shelter elsewhere. Damaged buildings are at risk of collapse, fires, or natural gas explosions. You should know where shelters might be located. They usually are set up in buildings that can hold many people, such as school gymnasiums or community centres. Keep in mind that it may take some time for emergency officials to find the safest building for a shelter.

After an earthquake, emergency workers may be too overwhelmed to help everyone. In many communities, people can take courses in earthquake safety. With proper training, ordinary citizens can help themselves and others.

To experience an earthquake in rural Alaska, turn to page 15.

To experience an earthquake in a city, turn to page 45.

For an island earthquake, turn to page 75.

Spring comes late in northern Alaska.

CHAPTER 2

Disaster in Alaska

The snow has been lightly falling all day. It's late March, but spring won't arrive for at least two months here in Alaska. You live in the remote woods several hours north of Anchorage. This time of year, the sun comes up late and goes down early. The chill lingers in the air for months.

You haven't had a lot of work lately. The construction business slows down in the winter. It will get busier in the summer. You pick up side jobs here and there when you can.

Just as you sit down to eat lunch, your phone rings. It's your friend Jeff.

15

Fishing is a major industry in Alaska.

"I just heard about some work on the docks in Valdez," he says. "Do you want to go?"

Valdez is a few hours away. You prefer to work closer to home. You look at your dog, Buddy. You hate leaving him behind for that long. But you know dock work pays well, even though the work is hard.

"Let me think about it."

"OK," Jeff says. "Call me back soon. I plan to leave in a few hours."

To go to Valdez, turn to page **18**.

To stay home, turn to page **19**.

You pick up the phone to call Jeff. "OK, let's go. My neighbour said he'd look after my dog."

On the drive, you look out of the window at the majestic mountains and thick stands of trees. Alaska is a beautiful but wild place. There's a lot of wide-open spaces between the towns.

You arrive in Valdez late in the afternoon. "What should we do?" Jeff asks. "We could go down to the docks now and see if we can get some work, or we could get a motel room and start fresh in the morning."

If you wait until morning, there might not be any work left. You know of many people who have come here looking for work in the last few days. But you're awfully tired. A good night of rest will help you feel better.

To go to the docks right away, turn to page 22.

To check in at a motel, turn to page 26.

You call Jeff. "I'm going to stay home," you tell him. A few hours later, you're cooking dinner. You're in your kitchen near the oven when you hear a low rumbling. You grab the worktop as your cupboard doors fly open. Dishes and tins of food hit the floor. Beneath your feet, the ground is shaking violently. It's an earthquake!

Outside, trees are bending low to the ground and snapping, as if hit by strong winds. A large crack opens in the ground. The bricks in your chimney collapse. After several seconds, the quaking stops.

Earthquakes can create huge cracks in roads.

Turn the page.

The house is dark. You grab a torch from a drawer. You have made sure to buy only safety-tested torches. You know they will work and will be safe in an emergency.

You look at the damage to your house. Several cracks have appeared in your walls. The kitchen is a mess, with broken dishes and food all over the floor. Your electricity is off. The gas for your oven and boiler is not working. Your house phone and mobile phone are both dead.

What should you do now? You don't have any heat or electricity. You wonder about the gas pipes. They may have been badly damaged, which could create a dangerous situation. The air in the house will soon turn cold, and you're not sure when help will arrive in this remote area.

You think about your neighbours Jane and Tom. They are in their 70s and have some health problems. Maybe you should try to check on them. But the roads are probably badly damaged.

To stay in your house, turn to page **29**.

To drive to the neighbours' house, turn to page **35**.

You head down to the docks, located on the edge of town on Prince William Sound. Valdez is a main fishing and shipping port in Alaska. Many goods first come into Valdez by ship and are taken into Alaska's interior by train or lorry. There might be some work unloading freight and fish from the ships and boats.

You spy a man with a clipboard at one of the docks.

"Excuse me," you say. "Do you know of any work around here? We work in construction, but we're laid off right now. We were hoping to get some work for a few days."

The man looks both of you up and down. "All right, you're in luck," he says gruffly. "Some of my men didn't show up today. We got a boat full of fish arriving in about half an hour. Can you stick around?"

"Of course!" you say. "Thanks a lot."

The boat comes in. You stand on the end of the dock with a few other men. Suddenly, the dock shifts below your feet and you hear a low rumbling sound. You look around. The dock is rippling up and down. You lose your balance and fall down.

"What's going on?" Jeff yells.

You look towards the town, and you watch buildings buckle and collapse. Trees are swaying and bouncing.

"It's an earthquake!" you scream as the dock below you collapses, spilling you and the rest of the men into the water. You inhale sharply as the icy water hits your skin. The fishing boat slams into part of the dock. You hear men scream in pain.

Turn the page.

"Jeff! Jeff!" you yell frantically, treading water as you scan the area. But there's no sign of him. Your arms and legs feel like blocks of ice. If you don't get to the shore now, you will be too cold to make it. You use all your strength to swim to the shore and pull yourself out of the water. Other men gather ropes and life jackets to rescue the ones who were sucked into the bay. You can't see Jeff, though. Where could he be?

Police officers and firefighters arrive after a few minutes. They gather rescue equipment and prepare to go into the water. An officer checks on you.

"We need you to evacuate," she says. "The town isn't safe. We're at risk for aftershocks, and it's likely that we'll get a tsunami within a few minutes. This is a very dangerous situation."

"But my friend is in the water!" you say. "I want to stay here until he's found!"

"We have a rescue team going in," she says. "We'll find your friend. You need to leave now."

You know you can help find Jeff. You could tell rescuers exactly where he went in. But the police officer is right. Maybe you should leave the rescue effort to the professionals.

To follow the officer's advice to evacuate, turn to page 32.

To stay, turn to page 37.

"Let's get some rest tonight and start fresh tomorrow," you say.

"Sounds good to me," Jeff says.

You drive to a motel. You check into the room and start unpacking when the floor starts to shake violently beneath your feet. Jeff says, "What's going on?"

A lamp on the table falls to the floor, and cracks appear in the walls. A loud rumbling sound fills your ears. The ground continues to shift beneath you.

Unsecured furniture becomes a safety hazard during an earthquake.

"It's an earthquake!" you yell. "It feels like the building is going to collapse! Let's get out of here!"

You and Jeff run outside. Trees sway back and forth. One falls on Jeff's van, crushing it. Windows break and shards of glass fall to the ground. The force of the quake knocks you to your knees. You both curl up, trying to protect your bodies from falling debris.

After a few seconds, the shaking stops. Everything is quiet. Then sirens start to sound. Rescue efforts are underway. A police car travels down the street and stops in front of you. When the officer hears that you ran out of the motel during the quake, he scolds you. "Don't you know that is one of the most dangerous things you can do?"

"I guess we panicked," Jeff replies. "Do you know where a shelter is located?"

Turn the page.

"Head to the primary school," the officer says. "We hear that building was not damaged. Volunteers will set up a shelter there."

At the school, you sit down next to a group of people and overhear them talking about leaving town. They are heading towards Anchorage, a couple of hours away.

"Do you have room in your car for two more?" you ask the driver, Joe.

"Sure, you're welcome to come with us," Joe says. "We just haven't decided which way to go. The roads are probably damaged. They might soon be closing the main roads. It might be best to take the smaller, inland roads. The police don't have the resources to block off every road. What do you guys think?"

To take the inland route, turn to page **39**.

To take the main road to Anchorage, turn to page **40**.

It's best to stay where you are. You saw the large cracks in the earth around your house. This is a rugged area. The roads are surrounded by rocky hillsides. An aftershock could easily trigger a landslide.

You shut off the gas pipes to the house. The propane tank outside, which supplies gas to your oven and boiler, may have been damaged. The gas pipes underneath the ground could be broken. Gas leaks could cause an explosion.

Without heat, it will get cold soon. You gather thick clothing and blankets. After a few hours, despite the thick layers, you are still very cold. Now it's dark, and you're sure you don't want to venture out into the unknown. But when will help arrive?

Turn the page.

You shiver uncontrollably. You decide to start a fire in the fireplace, forgetting that your chimney is damaged. You don't realize that you are in the first stages of hypothermia. The cold is affecting your ability to make good decisions.

You gather newspapers and firewood you have stacked in your porch. You light a match and are pleased at the warmth that comes from the fireplace. Soon you have a roaring fire going. But after a few minutes, smoke starts to fill the house. You cough and your eyes water. You feel your way to the doorway and stumble out of the front door. Buddy, your dog, follows you. Outside, you take deep breaths of the cold air.

After a few moments, a van drives up to your house. It's Jack, your nearest neighbour, who lives a few kilometres away.

"Are you OK?" Jack asks. "I thought I'd check on the neighbours. Who knows when emergency crews will arrive?"

"Yes, I'm OK, except I built a fire and now the house is full of smoke. I'm going to collect some snow to put out the fire."

"Forget about the house," Jack says. "Come with me where it's safe."

"I'm not sure it's any safer on the roads," you say. "An aftershock could occur at any moment. Besides, the fire is pretty small. It won't take much to put it out."

To go with Jack, turn to page 41.

To put out the fire, turn to page 42.

The police officer helps you get up. "You need to get moving," she says. "Head towards the town. You'll find relief workers who can get you into some dry clothes."

You take a moment to glance back at the water. Rescue boats are already in the bay, looking for survivors. The officer pushes you forward. "Let's go," she says. You think about sprinting towards the water, but you're too tired. She tells you to go to the primary school, where a shelter has been set up. You shiver as you walk slowly towards the school.

In the school gymnasium, volunteers are setting up camp beds and tables. Much to your relief, you see Jeff!

"Rescue workers pulled me out of the water right away," he says. "I was so scared."

You give him a hug. "I'm so glad you're all right. Let's sit down and warm up."

A group of people is talking next to you.

"We're going to head out of town," a man called Joe says. "We don't feel safe here. We're going to head back towards Anchorage."

"Do you have room in your car for two more?" you ask Joe. "We live near Anchorage, and our van is back at the dock."

"Sure," Joe says. "Let's go."

Anchorage, Alaska, was the site of a 9.2-magnitude earthquake in March 1964.

Turn the page.

A few of you pile into a van. "Which way should we go?" asks Joan, Joe's wife. "I heard the relief workers say that many of the main roads and bridges are damaged."

"Well, we could take the main road and see how far we get," you say. "But it might be faster to take some of the smaller roads inland. It's a little out of our way, but maybe they weren't as badly damaged as the roads near the coast."

As a group, you have to decide. What would be the best way to leave Valdez?

To take the inland route, turn to page 39.

To take the main road, turn to page 40.

You load Buddy into your van and head to Jane and Tom's. You want to make sure they're OK. You're glad to see the road is in fairly good shape. You have to dodge a few cracks in the road and some boulders, but you're able to pass through.

Jane and Tom are safe in their house.

"We're going to wait here for a few hours in case there are more aftershocks," Tom says. "Then we're going to drive to Anchorage and find a shelter."

A 1994 earthquake destroyed an overpass in California, USA.

Turn the page.

"That's a good idea," you say. "It's too cold to stay here for long. We don't want to build a fire in case a natural gas pipe has been broken." You all gather blankets and huddle together to keep warm through the night. At the first daylight, you drive towards Anchorage.

Your survival instincts have paid off. You stayed safe and lived through a major earthquake.

THE END

To follow another path, turn to page 13.
To read the conclusion, turn to page 101.

You find rescue workers launching boats into the water.

"Over there!" You point to where you last saw Jeff. "My friend went into the water right over there. Please try to find him!"

You watch the boat zigzag slowly through the water. The rescue workers come up with nothing. You're starting to feel desperate. Will they ever find Jeff? Is he even still alive?

You hear a crackle from a rescue worker's two-way radio. "Everybody leave the area!" the voice says. "A tsunami is heading this way!"

"Get back to shore!" the worker screams into the radio at the boats in the water. The boats start to quickly come to shore. Still no sight of Jeff. The worker looks at you. "Get out of here! It's not safe!" he yells.

Turn the page.

You turn around and see a huge wave about 60 metres high. It's headed straight for you! You try to run, but it's too late. The wall of water slams the shore and sweeps you away, along with everyone else on the shore and in the harbour. You all become victims of the deadly tsunami.

THE END

To follow another path, turn to page 13.
To read the conclusion, turn to page 101.

The group decides to take the less travelled roads. You plan to head north for a while, then turn to go west towards Anchorage. You are surprised that the roads are in fairly good shape. Going the inland route was the right choice.

After several hours you arrive in Anchorage. Police officers on the edge of town direct you to a shelter. There you find warm food and a bed. You queue up to use a phone to call your family. In the next day or so, law enforcement officers will escort you to your home to check on the damage. You have safely made it through the earthquake and its aftermath.

THE END

To follow another path, turn to page 13.
To read the conclusion, turn to page 101.

Your group decides to take the main road. A queue of vehicles heads out of Valdez. The roads are damaged but passable. The earthquake's force amazes you. Parts of the road have shifted entirely. Outside of the van's window, you notice that train carriages in the railway station have flipped on their sides.

At one of the bridges, traffic slows. Some drivers are turning their cars around because they think the bridge is unsafe. Joe keeps going forwards. When you're on the bridge, you hear a low rumble. "What's that noise?" one of the women asks. It takes you a second to realize what's happening.

"It's an aftershock!" you yell.

The quaking has caused a large crack in the bridge. Seconds later, the van plunges into the water. You are one of many casualties in this Alaska earthquake.

THE END

To follow another path, turn to page 13.
To read the conclusion, turn to page 101.

"I really think you should come with me," Jack says. "The house just isn't safe."

You look at your dog and then look at the house. You worry that the fire could get of control, but you know you can't go back in there. "You're right, Jack. Let's go."

The roads here are remote, but overall there isn't as much damage as you feared. A few kilometres down the road, you reach the house of your neighbours Tom and Jane. To your relief, they are not hurt.

"Jump in," Jack tells them. "Let's go to Anchorage. We can take a more inland route. Roads should be less damaged there. We can find a shelter and let our families know we're OK."

THE END

To follow another path, turn to page 13.
To read the conclusion, turn to page 101.

You are still worried about your house, but at least you and Buddy are safe.

"Jack, the fire is really small. Just help me get some snow, and I know I can put it out."

Jack agrees to help you. Both of you collect snow in 20-litre buckets you have in your garage. When the buckets are filled, you go into the house.

"I'm going to stay out here," Jack says. Buddy stays behind too.

When you get into the house, there's much more smoke than before. You go to the fireplace and dump the snow on the fire, but to your dismay, you see that it has spread to nearby furniture. There's now a fully fledged blaze in your house.

You start to gasp from the thick smoke. You can't see in front of you. Blindly, you try to feel your way out of the house, but you collapse a metre from the front door.

You can hear Jack yelling your name outside the door, but you know it's too late for him to save you. A damaged house after an earthquake is a dangerous place to be. Staying here has cost you your life.

THE END

To follow another path, turn to page 13.
To read the conclusion, turn to page 101.

The Bay Bridge connects San Francisco to Oakland, California.

CHAPTER 3

Earthquake in the city

Your working day is almost over. You pack your laptop in your bag and leave the newspaper office in San Francisco. As you head out of the door, your mobile phone rings. It's your best friend, Ann. "I'm having a few people over for dinner tonight," she says. "Why don't you join us?"

You pause for a moment before answering. You've been on the go all day. You would love to spend time with friends, but you would like to go home and change into comfortable clothes first.

"What time?"

"Come over right away," Ann says. "I know you too well. If you go home first, you will probably stay there all night!"

45

Turn the page.

She's right. Ann lives in the market district of the city. You live in Oakland, several kilometres away across the bay.

"Let me call you back in a few minutes," you tell her.

To go home, go to page 47.

To go to your friend's house, turn to page 51.

You call Ann back. "I'm just going to head home. It's been a long day. Let's get together this weekend."

In your car, you notice how the reddish-orange light from the sunset reflects in the water of the bay as you drive across the bridge. It's a beautiful day. Not a cloud in the sky, and hardly any wind.

After you cross the bridge, you're on the interstate highway when you see the strangest thing. The road before you is rippling up and down, like an ocean wave. Cars ahead of you hurtle into the air and come crashing back down onto the pavement. It's an earthquake! The screeching sound of metal on the roadway fills your ears. You hit the brakes hard when you feel the road below you give way.

You're on the top level of a two-level interstate. Before you know it, the top level crashes down onto the lower level. You scream in horror as you fall.

Turn the page.

The Cypress Freeway in Oakland, USA, collapsed during a 1989 earthquake.

Your stomach feels like it's on a roller coaster. Your car hits the roadway with a loud thump. You're stunned, but nothing seems to be broken or badly injured. You have survived an earthquake – so far. But aftershocks could arrive at any moment.

You feel trapped and start to panic. All you can think about is getting out of this small space. You try to open your car door, but it's stuck. You bang your shoulder against the door a couple of times, and it flies open. You tumble out of the car.

"Are you OK?" says a man who comes running up to your side.

"I … I … I think so," you stammer as you get to your feet.

Screams fill the air. You have escaped serious injury, but several others have not. You look around at the destruction. Cars are crumpled like balls of paper. Large sections of road have collapsed.

"My name is Ray, and I'm a firefighter," says the man who helped you. "Why don't you head to the secondary school a few blocks west? That school is a shelter in the city's emergency plan. If the school has been damaged, someone there will tell you where to go. But be careful. The earthquake has probably damaged power lines."

Turn the page.

"OK," you say, still dazed and in shock. Then a piercing scream gets your full attention. It's coming from below. "Help me! Help me!" a woman shouts.

Ray sprints to a spot in the road that has cracked open. He can see below to the lower level of the interstate. Other people run to his side.

"We have to get down there!" he shouts.

You could stay and help. You are small. Perhaps you could reach the woman more easily than the larger men who have gathered. But an aftershock could happen at any moment, further collapsing the road.

To stay and help rescue workers, turn to page 52.

To head to the shelter, turn to page 61.

You call Ann. "I'm coming over," you say. "I'll be there in about 20 minutes."

At Ann's house, you go into the kitchen and help her cut up fruit for dinner. Just then, the ground beneath you starts to shake. The cupboards fly open, and dishes crash to the floor. You grab the edge of the worktop to stay upright.

"It's an earthquake!" Ann screams. "What should we do?"

You try to think. You can either stay inside or run outside.

To stay inside, turn to page 56.

To run outside, turn to page 59.

The woman continues to scream. "Help me! Help me! I'm hurt!"

The screams are impossible to ignore. You run over to where the rescue group has gathered.

"That is a small space," Ray says, looking down below. "I'm not sure I can get down there."

"Let me go," you say.

You squeeze down into the hole. The jagged concrete rips through your clothes. There's barely enough room for your body, but you manage to wiggle down to the woman in the car.

"I can't get my door open!" cries the woman, who says her name is Tina.

You tug and pull at her car door, and it finally pops open. "Can you walk?" you ask.

"I think so," Tina says. "My arm and shoulder are really hurting, but I think I can walk."

Cars tumbled from the Bay Bridge during a 1989 earthquake.

You help Tina out of the car. You both walk to the opening where rescue workers wait above. You see Ray's arm reach down. Tina grabs his arm with her good arm, and you push her up from below. After she is safely on top, Ray grabs you and brings you up as well.

Turn the page.

"Thank you," he says. "It would have taken us a lot longer to get to her if you weren't here."

Just then, you hear a loud rumbling. The ground shakes and stirs. It's an aftershock! You all hang on to one another. The rumbling lasts for just a few seconds. But in that time, the road has collapsed even more. The opening that you just came through is now completely blocked.

Several injured people sit at the side of the road. They are hurt too badly to walk to the shelter. The rescue workers on the scene have to first try to reach people trapped in their vehicles. They are practising triage, where they help the most seriously injured people first.

"We need to get these people to a hospital," Ray says, pointing to the people sitting on the side of the road.

A man who arrived from a nearby house to offer help says, "I have a van. I can drive people to the hospital."

The man goes to get his van and returns a few minutes later. Ray turns to you. "We can use your help here," he says. "Or you could drive people to the hospital. Your choice."

To drive the injured people to the hospital,
*turn to page **68**.*

To stay and help rescue people,
*turn to page **69**.*

"Let's stay here!" you shout over the noise. Outside you see trees swaying and toppling. Both indoors and outdoors seem dangerous right now.

You and Ann take cover under a sturdy table. The ground continues to tremble and shake. You hear a loud roaring noise, like the earth is opening up all around you. You've never experienced anything like this.

Crack! You look up just in time to see a large chunk of plaster from the ceiling come crashing down. You made a good decision – the table protects you.

When the shaking is over, you get up and look around at the mess of broken dishes and spilled food. You slowly get to your feet.

You and Ann head outside and look at the damage. Houses have slid off their foundations. Trees are snapped in half. After a few moments of silence, the sound of sirens fills the air.

The 1989 7.1-magnitude earthquake in San Francisco caused £3.5 billion of damage.

Turn the page.

"What should we do now?" you ask. "I'm not sure the house is safe."

"We could stay and wait for rescue workers to tell us what to do next," Ann says. "Or we could try to find a shelter."

To stay at the house and wait for help, turn to page **64**.

To head to a shelter, turn to page **65**.

"I think we should go outside," you say.

You and Ann run out of the house. Trees are swaying. It's like an invisible hand is twisting them. Branches start to fall. One of them hits you and cuts you on the arm. A metre away, a large crack opens in the earth with a loud roar. You feel like you're going to be swallowed into the earth. The ground beneath you rolls like a wave.

After a few seconds, the shaking stops. All is quiet for a moment. Then dogs start to bark and you hear screams and cries in the distance. After a few more minutes, the blare of sirens fills the air.

"What now?" Ann asks. "We shouldn't go back into the house. The damage has probably made it unstable. We can wait here for help. Or we can start walking to see if we can find a shelter."

To stay at the house, turn to page 60.

To find an emergency shelter, turn to page 65.

"Maybe we should check on my neighbours," Ann says. "Marge and George live a couple of houses down. I want to make sure they're OK."

On the street, you have to walk around fallen tree branches and jump over cracks in the road. You reach the neighbours' house. Marge is outside crying.

"What's wrong?" Ann asks her. "Are you hurt?"

"I think my leg is broken," she says. "And George is inside. I think he may be trapped!"

Your first instinct is to go inside to find George. But you know the inside of a house is not a safe place to be after an earthquake. You could try to run and get help. Maybe there is an emergency crew nearby.

To go inside the house, turn to page 71.

To find an emergency crew, turn to page 72.

Other people with minor injuries stumble from their cars.

"A firefighter told me to head to the school," you tell them. "If the building is not damaged, aid workers there can help us. We can go as a group."

You take the arm of a woman. She says her name is Betty. She appears to be in her 70s and is having trouble walking. "I hurt my knee," Betty says. "I don't know how far I can go."

"Let's get off the road," you say. "I hear sirens below. Someone may be able to help us." You and Betty carefully pick your way through the crumbled concrete. The streets look like war zones you've seen on TV. Large cracks split the roads. Branches and limbs from toppled trees are strewn through the streets and gardens. Every house is damaged. Chimneys have fallen, and houses are twisted off their foundations.

Turn the page.

You've walked several blocks when you trip over a piece of debris. You drop Betty's arm as you land flat on your face on the hard concrete. "Ouch!" you cry. You've badly hurt your leg, and blood streams from a cut above your ear. You try to stand, but you can't seem to move.

"Are you all right?" Betty says.

"I think I twisted my ankle. And my head hurts." You hold your hand on the cut, trying to stop the flow of blood.

Betty starts yelling for help. Three teenage boys run over. "Don't worry, lady. We'll get you to the shelter." Two of the boys, Luke and Tyler, form a human chair with their arms to carry you. The other one, Jake, takes Betty's arm.

With the boys' help, you reach the school a short time later. Aid workers there get you the medical help you need. You're lucky that the boys were there – otherwise, the story could have ended very differently.

THE END

To follow another path, turn to page 13.
To read the conclusion, turn to page 101.

"Let's stay here," you say. "It seems safer."

Ann looks out of the window. "The streets look pretty damaged. I hope someone will come to check on us soon."

You go back inside. Ann gets some blankets. Without electricity, a chill creeps into the air.

It quickly becomes dark. "Let's light some candles," Ann says. She goes into the kitchen to get matches and comes back into the living room. She gathers some candles on a coffee table and strikes a match.

BOOM! The flash of bright light and cracking sound jolt you. You and Ann are blown backwards as the room fills with flames. In the earthquake, natural gas pipelines were cracked. Some of the invisible gas had filled the house. The match ignited the gas, and the resulting explosion cost both you and Ann your lives.

THE END

To follow another path, turn to page 13.
To read the conclusion, turn to page 101.

"Let's go to a shelter," you say. "We can try to get in touch with our families. I'm really worried about my mum and dad."

"But it's getting dark," Ann says. "I don't think it's a good idea to walk through the damage when we can't see."

"That's a good point," you say. "But we shouldn't go back into the house."

Fires blazed in San Francisco after an earthquake caused gas lines to rupture.

Turn the page.

"That's true. Let's put up a tent and camp out here tonight. We can try to find a shelter in the morning."

Ann has a tent and sleeping bags in her garage. You feel a lot safer staying in an open area. A couple of small aftershocks rattle in the night, but no more serious damage occurs.

At daylight, you and Ann pick your way through the debris-filled streets. You barely recognize the city. You have to scramble over fallen trees and jump over large cracks in the road.

You come across an ambulance crew. They are treating injured people.

"Can you let us know where we can find a shelter?" you ask. "I want to get in touch with my family."

"The school a couple of blocks down that way is an emergency shelter," says the emergency medical technician, pointing down the street. "Aid workers there will help you get in touch with your family."

At the shelter, workers have set up beds. A generator provides electricity.

They have mobile phones that work. You queue up to call your parents. They are safe. And so are you.

THE END

To follow another path, turn to page 13.
To read the conclusion, turn to page 101.

"I can drive to the hospital," you say. You and a few others help injured people into the van.

You have never seen such damage in your life. You dodge tree branches in the streets. In some areas, wide cracks have opened in the roads. Every bump and jolt causes the injured people to scream in pain.

You groan as you come to a junction that is completely blocked. You're only a short distance from the hospital. But you're stuck.

"We can't go any farther," you say. "Let me find some help. We're going to have to get you all to the hospital on foot."

In your hurry to get help, you step out of the van without looking at the ground. A downed power line is in the street, right in front of your foot. The jolt of electricity as you step on it stops your heart.

THE END

To follow another path, turn to page 13.
To read the conclusion, turn to page 101.

You start shaking from fear and adrenaline. You realize you're in no condition to drive. "I'll stay here," you say.

"Keep an eye on those people," the firefighter says to you, pointing to the injured people on the side of the road. "Let's keep them here. I don't want to take the chance of transporting them to the hospital. The roads are probably blocked by debris and dangerous. I've called other firefighting teams. More rescue workers will be on their way soon."

You stay with the injured people. Someone brings blankets from a nearby house. You keep the people warm and comfortable. About half an hour later, you hear sirens. The professional rescue workers have arrived. Emergency medical technicians, firefighters, and police officers attend to Tina and the rest of the injured people.

Turn the page.

After everyone is rescued and treated, you walk to a nearby shelter. You hope there will be a phone there that you can use to call Ann. A series of good decisions kept you safe and allowed you to help others as well.

THE END

To follow another path, turn to page 13.
To read the conclusion, turn to page 101.

"I'll go and get him," you say.

"Be careful!" Ann says. "There could be an aftershock any minute."

You wave off her concerns. You head into the house and find George trapped in the bedroom. A heavy dresser fell onto his leg. You're just a metre away from him when the house starts to shake again. It's an aftershock! The walls buckle and collapse around you. You fall down, and a piece of plaster falls on your head, killing you instantly.

THE END

To follow another path, turn to page 13.
To read the conclusion, turn to page 101.

"I'll go and look for help," you say.

You run down the street as fast as you can, but the debris slows you down. A small aftershock ripples through the street. You lose your balance, but you're not hurt. You find a police officer at an intersection.

"Can you please help me? A friend is trapped in a house!"

The officer nods his head and calls for emergency workers on his radio. He follows you to Marge and George's house. By the time you get there, emergency workers arrive. They go into the house and return a few minutes later with George strapped to a stretcher. He is hurt, but alive. You made a good decision in leaving the rescue work to the professionals.

THE END

To follow another path, turn to page 13.
To read the conclusion, turn to page 101.

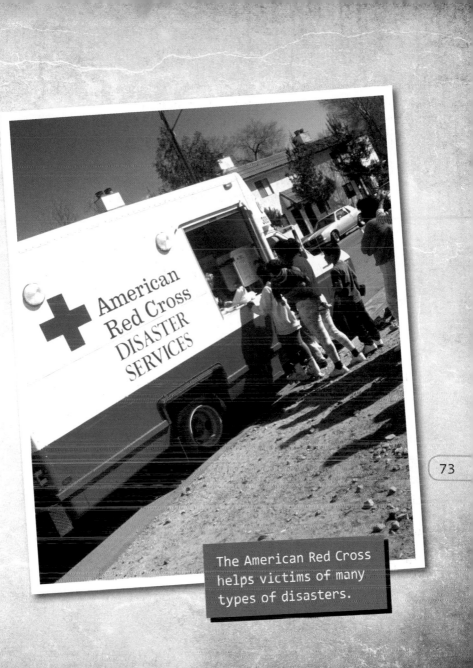

The American Red Cross helps victims of many types of disasters.

Sendai, Japan, is a city of about 1 million people.

CHAPTER 4

A quake and a big wave

It's a beautiful Friday morning in the city of Sendai, Japan. You gaze at the bright blue sky through your office window. You are ready for the weekend after a hard week at work. You hear a knock at your door.

"Come in," you say, as you finish typing a report on your computer.

It's your boss, Ren Sato. He sits down across from you. "I would like you to go to Fukushima for the afternoon. We have an important client there who needs some help. I think you are the best person to help him."

75

You sigh. You don't really want to go anywhere today. You promised your son that you would take him to the cinema tonight.

"I know it is a last-minute request. I apologize," Mr Sato says. "If you can't go, I will get someone else. But if you do it, I will appreciate it very much."

You want to keep your boss happy. But you've been looking forward to getting home, where your wife, Aiko, and son, Hideaki, wait.

To stay in Sendai, go to page 77.

To go to Fukushima, turn to page 79.

"I am going to stay here. But thank you for the offer," you tell Mr Sato.

You finish typing your report just before lunchtime. You grab your briefcase and head to your car to pick up some lunch.

At a traffic light, your car begins to shake. Oh no, you think. This is a new car. It had better not need repairs already.

But then your car begins to pitch and roll. It feels as if you're on a roller coaster. Even with your seat belt on, your body slams from side to side. Outside the car window, you see trees sway, utility poles topple and power lines swing. Shopfront windows explode, sending glass raining down into the street. It's an earthquake!

After several seconds the shaking stops. You get out of your car and see a group of frightened people gathered on the pavement. You join them.

Turn the page.

People in Sendai gathered in the streets after the earthquake on 11 March 2011.

"What should we do now?" a woman asks.

"I think we should head to higher ground," replies a man. "Japan is surrounded by sea. This was a massive quake. I wouldn't be surprised if a tsunami is on its way."

"But how will we get anywhere?" says another woman. "The roads are destroyed. We'll have to leave on foot. I'm sure there will be aftershocks. Moving in this mess may be very dangerous."

To move to higher ground, turn to page 82.

To stay on the street, turn to page 88.

"I will go to Fukushima," you tell Mr Sato. "Let me get my things."

After a train journey of a bit more than an hour, you arrive at your company's Fukushima office on the eighth floor of a high-rise building. You have just settled in when you feel a tremendous shaking. It's an earthquake!

You take shelter under a desk as you watch files, plants and computers crash to the floor. The building creaks and roars. You think it might collapse. Screams and cries fill the air.

The trembling stops after a few moments. Your co-workers gather together and try to calm down.

"I think it's best that we leave," says one co-worker, Keiko. "We don't want to be in this building if aftershocks hit."

Turn the page.

After a few minutes of walking, you hear sirens. Ambulances and police cars pick their way carefully through the damaged streets. Rescue efforts are under way. At a street corner, a police officer directs traffic.

"Head to the nearest school, about two blocks that way." She points up the street. "The school was not damaged. You can get first aid there. Food and bottled water will arrive shortly."

At the shelter, you take a seat. Some people nearby are talking.

"I don't want to stay," one man says. "I'm sure

the earthquake has damaged the nuclear reactors near the city. I'm going to leave as soon as possible."

"But where will you go? The roads are damaged," a woman tells him. "And more aftershocks may strike. You don't want to be on the road if that happens. We should listen to the aid workers here. They are telling people not to leave."

You want to get back to Sendai to check on your family. But Sendai is not safe. The city is on the coast of the Pacific Ocean and faces the threat of a tsunami. The man may be right about the damaged nuclear reactors. But trying to get home will not be a safe journey.

To head to Sendai, turn to page **85**.

To stay in Fukushima, turn to page **90**.

"Let's get moving," you say.

Your group heads to the part of the city located on the hilltop. At the top of a hill, you stop and listen. Besides the shouts and cries of people around you, you also hear a low rumbling. It sounds like a train.

The rumbling gets louder. You turn around and look back towards the coast. A huge black wall of water is heading towards you.

"It's a tsunami!" you yell. You're in front of a large building. A man in the doorway calls to you. "Come in here! We can go to the top floor. We'll be safest there!"

You all run into the building. You've never climbed stairs so quickly. You're almost to the top when the tsunami hits. The sound of the water hitting the building is deafening. A window near you shatters, cutting your skin.

Workers in Sendai scrambled to a factory roof to avoid the tsunami.

Turn the page.

After a few minutes everything becomes quiet. You've survived both an earthquake and a tsunami.

But you're bleeding badly from your cuts. You need to get help. Your cuts could become infected the longer you wait to go to a hospital. But you also need to find your wife and son. Your family has an emergency plan because you live in an earthquake zone. You agreed to go to the nearest shelter and stay there in case you were separated during an earthquake. If Aiko and Hideaki were looking for you, they would go to a shelter first.

*To go to the shelter, turn to page **86**.*

*To find a hospital, turn to page **92**.*

"Where are you headed?" you ask the man, whose name is Takumi. "I'm from Sendai and would like to get home as quickly as possible."

"I'm going to head inland," Takumi says. "I don't want to be anywhere near the coast for a while. But I heard some people over there say that they were going to Sendai." He points across the room. "I'll be happy to take you with me. I really think we'd all be safer if we go inland."

Takumi has a good point. You need to stay safe and healthy if you want to find your family. Sendai is probably still very dangerous. But you really want to make sure Aiko and Hideaki are OK.

To go to Sendai, turn to page 94.

To head inland, turn to page 95.

You bandage your cuts as best as you can with a first-aid kit you found in one of the offices. A cut on your left arm is very deep and will need stitches.

You walk out of the building with your group. The street is covered with several centimetres of water. The cold, dirty seawater soaks your shoes and trousers. You trip on debris and fall to the street. The salty water stings your cuts. Emergency sirens are blaring as rescue attempts begin. The city comes back to life as rescue crews try to help survivors.

There's a police car at the end of the block. "Excuse me," you say to the officer. "Where is the nearest shelter?"

"There's a school five blocks to the west," the officer says. "Go there and wait for help."

You make your way to the school. You begin to shiver, and your cuts are still bleeding. You start to feel dizzy and faint. First-aid workers help you to a chair. They wash your cuts and put new bandages on them.

You know you're supposed to stay at a shelter according to your family's emergency plan. But what if Aiko and Hideaki are trapped in your house and can't get to a shelter?

To go to the house, turn to page **97**.

To stay at the shelter, turn to page **99**.

You wait on the street. One co-worker, Yoko, has deep cuts on her legs from flying glass. She can't walk, and you don't want to leave her.

Just then, the earth starts to shake again. You all grab one another and hang on. The aftershock is less severe than the earthquake, but you're still frightened. After it's over, you sit on the kerb.

"What's that noise?" says one of the men. It sounds like a low rumbling, like a train. The ground shakes ever so slightly. There's a hill nearby. You scramble up the hillside and look towards the sea.

What you see frightens you to your very core. Past the beach, you see what looks like a moving, swirling, black wall. It comes closer and closer. It's a tsunami, and there's no escape. "The water is coming!" you scream. "Everyone, move higher!

You and your co-workers try to get up the hill, but Yoko slows you down. The roar of the huge wave fills your ears.

In March 2011 a massive earthquake triggered a tsunami in Japan.

Within moments, the water crashes around you. You hang on to a tree trunk with all your might. You hold your breath as the water hits you like a liquid brick wall. You cling desperately to the tree, but the force of the water tears you away. You are one of thousands the tsunami claims that day.

THE END

To follow another path, turn to page 13.
To read the conclusion, turn to page 101.

It's best to stay at the shelter until you learn if the roads are safe. You are talking to some people a few hours later when the rescue workers make an announcement.

"We just learned that the Fukushima nuclear plant is seriously damaged. We need to evacuate everything in a 20-kilometre radius. We have arranged transport to shelters a few miles away. Stay inside until the buses arrive. You will be exposed to less radiation if you stay inside the building."

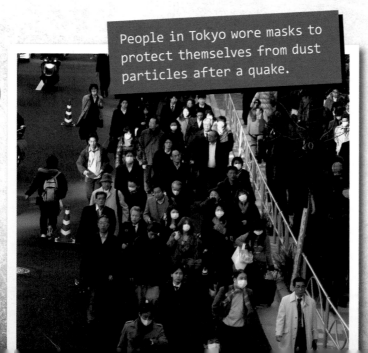

People in Tokyo wore masks to protect themselves from dust particles after a quake.

You can't see the radiation from the nuclear plant, but you know it's out there. Even indoors, you feel at risk. You should have left when you had the chance.

You arrive at the new shelter. After a couple of days, you are able to make it back home to Sendai and are reunited with your family. But the radiation has long-lasting effects that won't show up for several years. You survived the earthquake, but your health is permanently damaged because of that day in Fukushima.

THE END

To follow another path, turn to page 13.
To read the conclusion, turn to page 101.

You walk outside. Several centimetres of dirty, cold seawater fill the streets. After taking a few steps, you stumble. The dirty water washes over your wounds.

The sound of sirens fills the air. Rescue efforts are under way. A police officer stands on the corner.

"Do you know if the hospital is open?" you ask.

"Yes. It was damaged, but they are treating patients there."

You head to the hospital, where they give you antibiotics. You are at a high risk of infection because of the dirty water entering your wounds.

"You made a good decision to get treated right away," the doctor says. "I think we will see some very serious illnesses within a couple of days. Many people are badly injured."

At the hospital, you put your name on a list of survivors. The list will go to many shelters so people can check on loved ones.

After a few hours, you get a welcome surprise. It's Aiko and Hideaki! They saw your name on a list and came to find you. You have survived the earthquake and tsunami with your health and family intact.

THE END

To follow another path, turn to page 13.
To read the conclusion, turn to page 101.

You find the people heading to Sendai. They agree to take you with them.

"Let's take the back roads," the driver, Hana, says. "I'm sure they have shut down the main roads already."

You head out of town. Very few cars are on the road. You have to travel slowly because the roads are badly damaged. A few kilometres out of Fukushima, you feel a rumbling. The van skids.

"It's an aftershock!" Hana screams.

You hit your head on the window. The road buckles in front of you and sends the van spinning into the ditch. The van rolls over and lands upside down. You hear moans from the other passengers before everything goes black. The car crash has taken your life.

THE END

To follow another path, turn to page 13.
To read the conclusion, turn to page 101.

"I think you're right," you tell Takumi. "Let's go inland."

You walk a few blocks to Takumi's house, even though you know going outside puts you at a high risk of radiation exposure. But you want to get out of town as soon as possible. At Takumi's house, you both get into his car. The roads directly outside of Fukushima are heavily damaged, and you must travel slowly. But the farther inland you go, the better the roads are. Several kilometres away from Fukushima, you notice the damage in the country is much less.

You decide to stop in a town about 80 kilometres away. At a small café, you see a young woman with a computer.

"Excuse me, could I borrow your computer?" you ask her. "I just came from Fukushima, and I want to try to contact my wife in Sendai. I left my mobile phone at the office."

Turn the page.

"I just read that someone has set up a people finder online," she says. "You could type in your name and say that you're OK."

You find the site and type in your information. A few hours later, you check back in. Thankfully, Aiko posted a message! She and Hideaki are OK. You leave her a message to come to you, where she and Hideaki will be safe. You will find a place to stay here until it is safe to return to your home in Sendai.

THE END

To follow another path, turn to page 13.
To read the conclusion, turn to page 101.

Your house is about a 15-minute walk away. You wade through streets flooded with water and debris. You trip several times, and your bandages work loose. Water gets into your cuts. But you must get home and check on your family.

When you get to the house, no one is there. You can only hope that Aiko and Hideaki have gone to a shelter. You probably should have stayed there.

You are shocked at the devastation you see. Several centimetres of water cover the first floor. Dishes have tumbled out of the cupboards. Food from your pantry is spilled onto the floor. Upstairs, furniture is tipped over. Your television fell to the floor during the quake and is smashed. Cracks appear in the walls.

You head back to the shelter to find your family. But your cuts are still bleeding heavily. You start to feel weak and dizzy. You make it through the shelter doors and then collapse.

Turn the page.

When you wake up, you are at the hospital. You are in pain, but you are relieved to see Aiko and Hideaki at your bedside.

"You have been in a coma for several days," Aiko said. "An infection settled into your legs. Doctors had to amputate your left foot in order to save your life."

You have survived. But your decision to leave the shelter when you did has changed your life forever.

THE END

To follow another path, turn to page 13.
To read the conclusion, turn to page 101.

You decide it would be best to stay here and wait for Aiko and Hideaki. A doctor looks at your wounds. "I'm going to start you on antibiotics," she says. "Your cuts were exposed to seawater, which is full of bacteria. You could get a serious infection."

You take the medicine and fall asleep. When you wake up, you look for Aiko and Hideaki, but they are still not here. A rescue worker puts your name on a list. The list will be sent to all the shelters to help reunite families. After two days of stress and worry, a rescue worker says to you, "Your wife and son are safe. They are at a shelter a few kilometres away. They will be here soon."

When Aiko and Hideaki arrive, you all get on a bus to the city where your parents live. After a series of good decisions, you have all survived.

THE END

To follow another path, turn to page 13.
To read the conclusion, turn to page 101.

An 8.8-magnitude earthquake destroyed a road in Chile in 2010.

CHAPTER 5

Surviving an earthquake

Do you have what it takes to survive an earthquake? Earthquake survivors are alert and prepared. They know where danger lurks. Inside buildings, familiar objects such as unsecured furniture and electronic equipment can become deadly missiles. Trees and power lines outdoors pose threats. Bridges and overpasses may collapse. And at the beach, a tsunami can sweep away everything in its path.

A pre-earthquake plan can help you make good decisions when disaster strikes. Find the places in every room where you can drop, cover and hold on. Get first-aid and CPR training.

You and your family members also should choose a meeting place in case you get separated. Even if your house appears to be safe after an earthquake, you should plan to seek safe shelter elsewhere. Natural gas leaks and other invisible threats in your home can be present for days or weeks after a quake.

The last thing you want to do is to scramble for important items such as shoes and torches during an earthquake. A packed disaster kit will save valuable time and may even save your life.

If you have to go to a shelter, what should you bring? The US Geological Survey recommends taking the following items with you to a shelter:

- Your own bottled water, food and snacks.

- Items for sleeping, such as a pillow, blankets and an air mattress or pad.

- Any needed medicines.

- Extra clothes, including warm clothes such as jackets.

- Bathroom supplies, such as a towel, flannel, toothpaste and toothbrush.

- Identification and insurance information.

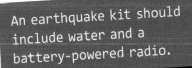

An earthquake kit should include water and a battery-powered radio.

Most emergency shelters don't allow pets, so you will need to have a plan in place for your pet as well. These items should be part of that plan:

- Find out if there is an emergency shelter where you can take your pet in case of a disaster.

- Keep your pet up to date on its vaccinations.

- Make sure your pet wears a collar with your name, address and phone number on it, or have your pet microchipped.

Once you are able to return to your home, you must concentrate on getting your life back in order. This process can be more stressful than the earthquake itself. People need time to heal from the massive changes an earthquake can cause. It can be weeks before power is restored and clean drinking water is available. Buildings you are used to seeing might be destroyed. You may have to find other ways to get around because of damaged roads.

Most of all, earthquake survival depends on staying calm. You must be prepared and make smart decisions based on what you know about earthquakes and their dangers. Many people have survived major earthquakes. With the right knowledge and decisions, you can be one of them.

REAL SURVIVORS

Miracle baby

One of the tiniest survivors of the 11 March 2011
Japanese earthquake and tsunami was a 4-month-
old baby girl. She was swept away from her
parents when the tsunami waters flooded their
house in Ishinomaki. For three days, her parents
thought she was dead. But rescue workers heard
a cry in the rubble and found her. No one knows
how she survived the damage, but she proved that
miracles can occur even amid disaster.

Alaska survivor

Eleven-year-old Paul Timothy "Timmy" Selanoff
was walking along the shore near Chenega,
Alaska, on 27 March 1964, when a huge
earthquake struck. Timmy dodged quaking
boulders as he ran for safety on top of a cliff.
There he watched massive tsunami waves wipe
out his village. All that was left was the school.
Twenty-six people from Chenega died that day
– one-quarter of the village's population. The
victims included Tommy's brother and sister.

Trapped in rubble

When a 7.0 magnitude earthquake struck the Caribbean nation of Haiti on 12 January 2010, many people were trapped in collapsed buildings. One of those trapped was 47-year-old American Rick Santos. He and four co-workers were in the lobby of the Hotel Montana in the city of Port-au-Prince when it collapsed around them. They were trapped for three nights, but were protected by the lobby's huge front desk. The only food they had was one lollipop, which they shared. Santos and two co-workers were rescued and survived. The two other co-workers died.

Deadly tsunami

When a massive underwater earthquake struck off the coast of Indonesia on 26 December 2004, it unleashed a tsunami that killed more than 200,000 people. TV presenter Nate Berkus was on holiday in Sri Lanka with his friend Fernando Bengoechea. The two were in a small hut near the shore when the tsunami hit. Berkus and Bengoechea were washed out in the swirling waters. Berkus managed to swim to a fence and climb to a rooftop, where he was safe. Bengoechea was never found and is believed dead.

SURVIVAL QUIZ

1. The safest place to be during an earthquake is:
A. On a bridge.
B. On a pavement next to a tall building.
C. Underneath a piece of sturdy furniture,
   such as a table.
D. Outside near a large tree.

2. Earthquakes are more likely in the Ring of Fire;
which ocean does this surround?
A. Pacific Ocean
B. Atlantic Ocean
C. Indian Ocean
D. Arctic Ocean

3. Which scale is used to measure the strength of
earthquakes?
A. Mighty Scale
B. Smith Scale
C. Richter Scale
D. Big Scale

Answers: C, A, C

READ MORE

Earthquakes (Eyewitness Disaster), Helen Dwyer (Franklin Watts, 2011)

Earth-shattering Earthquakes, Anita Ganeri (Scholastic, 2010)

Extreme Survival (100 Facts), Jen Green (Miles Kelly, 2010)

The Ultimate Survival Guide (The Science of…), Mike Flynn (Pan Macmillan, 2010)

WEBSITES

www.earthquakes.bgs.ac.uk/education/home.html
Find out more about earthquakes, particularly in the United Kngdom.

www.geolsoc.org.uk/Plate-Tectonics
Learn about plate tectonics on this website.

news.bbc.co.uk/1/hi/world/americas/8459653.stm
Visit this web page to find out how survivors are found after an earthquake.

GLOSSARY

aftershock (AF-tur-shok)   a small earthquake that follows a larger one

antibiotic (an-ti-bye-OT-ik)   a drug that kills bacteria and is used to cure infections and disease

debris (DE-bree)   the remains of something that has been destroyed

landslide (LAND-slide)   a large mass of earth and rocks that suddenly slides down a mountain or hill

magnitude (MAG-ni-tewd)   a measure of the amount of energy released by an earthquake

nuclear reactor (NEW-klee-ur ree-AK-tuhr)   a device that maintains and controls nuclear reactions to create power and energy

radiation (ray-dee-AY-shuhn)   tiny particles sent out from radioactive material

Richter scale (RIK-tuhr SKALE)   a scale that measures the power of an earthquake

tectonic (tek-TON-ik)   pertaining to Earth's crust

tsunami (tsoo-NAH-mee)   a large, destructive wave caused by an underwater earthquake

BIBLIOGRAPHY

A Day of Horror: The March 11, 2011 Japan Earthquake – A Foreigner's Perspective, Bradley Lobue (Amazon Digital Services, 2012)

"Earthquake in Japan: A Race Against Time", Barbara Demick, Laura King and Mark Magnier (*Los Angeles Times*, 13 March 2011)

"Hundreds Dead in Huge Quake", Randy Shilts and Susan Sward (*San Francisco Chronicle*, 18 Oct. 1989)

"The Dramas on I-880: People Who Were There.", Susan Michael Robertson (*San Francisco Chronicle*, 21 Oct. 1989)

The Great Alaska Earthquake, March 27, 1964. Stan Cohen (Pictorial Histories Pub. Co., 1995)

United States Geological Survey Earthquake Hazards Program 2012. 1 Nov. 2012.
http://earthquake.usgs.gov/earthquakes

United States Geological Survey Putting Down Roots in Earthquake Country 2011.
1 Nov. 2012. www.earthquakecountry.info/roots/ PuttingDownRootsSoCal2011.pdf

INDEX